HEAD-SMASHED-IN BUFFALO JUMP

GORDON REID

FIFTH
HOUSE

First published in 1992 by Boston Mills Press
Revised edition published in 2002 by Fifth House Ltd.

Design by John Luckhurst / GDL
Front cover painting by Ivan Kocsis
Back cover painting by Milton Achtimichuk
All scans by St. Solo Computer Graphics Inc.

The publisher gratefully acknowledges the support of
The Canada Council for the Arts and the Department of
Canadian Heritage. We acknowledge the financial support
of the Government of Canada through the Book Publishing
Industry Development Program for our publishing activities.

Printed in Canada by Friesens

9 8 7 6 5 4 3 2

National Library of Canada Cataloguing in Publication Data

Reid, Gordon, 1954-
  Head-Smashed-In Buffalo Jump

  Includes bibliographical references.
  ISBN 1-894004-83-3

  1. Buffalo jump—Alberta. 2. Indians of North America—
    Alberta—Antiquities.
  3. Excavations (Archaeology)—Alberta. 4. Head-Smashed-In
    Buffalo Jump
  Provincial Historic Site (Alta.) 5. Alberta—Antiquities. I. Title.

  E78.A34R45 2002   971.23'4   C2002-910197-2

Fifth House Ltd.
A Fitzhenry & Whiteside Company

1-800-387-9776
www.fitzhenry.ca

Images courtesy:

page 32 – Milton Achtimichuk
page 5 – Jack Brink
pages 9, 29, 30, 37 – Laura Draper
page 34 – *Fort Macleod Gazette*
page 24 – Glenbow Museum
pages ii, 14, 20, 32 – Head-Smashed-In Buffalo Jump
pages 1, 4, 7, 18 – Ivan Kocsis
pages 8, 16 – John Luckhurst
pages 8, 13, 26, 27, 28, 31, 35, 36, 39 – Gordon Reid

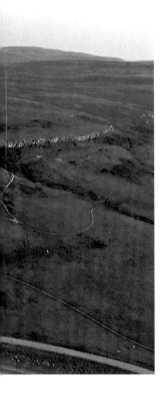

CONTENTS

PART ONE

THE BUFFALO AND THE NATIVE PEOPLES

The Hunter and the Hunted

In warmer months the buffalo grazed the open prairie, but in winter they sought shelter in the valleys of the foothills. This disappearing act generated many Native myths. Some tribes believed that the buffalo went underground in autumn and that they could often be heard fighting

below the prairie. A related tale had it that the Earth Mother sheltered buffalo spirits in an underworld home. During times of famine, the Natives prayed to the Earth Mother and she dispatched co-operative souls to inhabit the bodies of unsuspecting buffalo. These souls led the bison to Native camps and thus provided food for the hungry tribe.

One tribal legend claimed that the buffalo emerged each spring from the depths of great caverns in what is now northwest Texas, while another tribe thought the bison wintered beneath a mysterious lake. (This tale may have had root in the fact that buffalo are good swimmers and do not fear water.)

Bison are hardy mammals and are able to find food even under deep blankets of snow. Their physical bulk and thick hides protect them against icy prairie winds and blizzards. Also, buffalo cows retain an inch or more of fat during the winter months. The thick winter coats are shed in late spring, when the buffalo remove woolly patches by rubbing against trees, shrubbery, and rocks.

The average adult male buffalo weighs 700–800 kilograms (1700 pounds) and has permanent, curved horns on a large, bearded head. They stand 1.5–1.8 metres (5–6 feet) tall at the shoulder hump,

A sketch by John Mix Stanley from 1853 shows how the buffalo covered the plains in the mid-nineteenth century. Courtesy Glenbow Archives NA-1274-2.

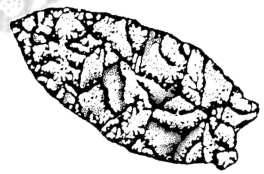

and range from 2.1–3.7 metres (7–12 feet) in length. Wood bison are slightly larger than the plains variety, and their hair is somewhat shorter and darker brown. Female bison are smaller than males, and their horns, though approximately the same length, are sharper and slimmer than those of the males.

Buffalo once freely roamed the North American prairies in herds varying in size from a few hundred to over one thousand animals. They often blocked railway lines in the early American west. Canadian historian Fraser Symington wrote, "A herd could literally travel five hundred miles in a straight line and not be stopped by any natural obstacle. Conversely a herd could wander anywhere, and usually did—an erratic drift which this month brought bounty beyond imagining to an Indian band and next month left the surrounding plain barren."

Native hunters did not take the buffalo for granted. Elaborate rituals and ceremonies were created to ensure the return of the herds. "Buffalo-calling" ceremonies were used by several tribes.

Artist and traveller George Catlin (1796–1872) noted that when the buffalo moved from familiar grazing grounds, the Indians were quick to take action. The swiftest runners raced through the village to announce the start of a buffalo dance. Moments later the dance commenced in the centre of the village, in front of the medicine lodge. In the Dakota Mandan ceremony, fifteen or more braves danced about vigorously, outfitted in buffalo hides, horned headgear, and masks. The tribesmen each held their best hunting lances and bows.

The dance sometimes lasted for two or three weeks, with the din of drums and rattles, yells and songs resounding across the prairie landscape. Masked spectators stood ready to replace fatigued dancers as they left the circle. A respected Mandan elder sang,

Many buffalo I hear,
They are coming now,
They are coming now,
Sharpen your arrows,
Sharpen your knives!

While the dance progressed, braves scouted the nearby hills for signs of buffalo. When the bison were sighted, the signal was given by the throwing off of robes, and the Great Spirit, the medicine men, and the dancers were thanked for their participation in the successful dance.

A variation of the Mandan buffalo dance was a religious feast and ceremony heralding the return of buffalo-hunting season. In this ceremony, eight braves wearing painted buffalo skins imitated the actions of the bison. The dancers began the ritual by standing at the tips of four canoes which were positioned to represent the four points of the compass. The medicine men knew that the buffalo might appear from any of the four corners of the world. Two braves dressed as grizzly bears threatened the dancers, but these symbolic predators were lured away by offers of food. As older tribesmen prayed and beat rhythmically on corn sacks, another brave, disguised as the demon spirit Famine, entered the circle, only to be driven out with stones and loud curses.

Catlin said that during the buffalo-calling ceremonies, "The rites and incantations were continued until the buffalo did come; whereby the medicine men acquired merit, and in this way 'never failed.'"

The buffalo was a central part of Plains Indian folklore. The Sioux and Pawnee believed a buffalo guarded the gate to the mortal world. In the words of Pawnee elder Black Elk, "A Cosmic Buffalo, Father and Grandfather of the universe, stands at the gate through which the animals come forth onto this earth, and back through which they return to be reborn; also, that in the course of a cycle of four world ages, this Buffalo drops one hair with the passage of each year, and with the passage of each age, one leg. The Buffalo has twenty-eight ribs, and in our war bonnets we have twenty-eight feathers. The sundance lodge has twenty-eight enclosing parts, all resting on the central tree. Twenty-eight is the number of days of the moon's growing and dying."

Some tribes worshipped an albino buffalo cow. Bleached bison skulls were thought to be good medicine and were piled up to entice wandering herds for a future hunt.

Hunters came to know "wallows" (circular depressions) as a sign of plentiful bison. Wallows are created by repetitive pawing at the dry earth. Buffalo strike the ground with their hoofs and horns prior to rolling or "wallowing." Bulls are more prone to wallowing than cows, but on a hot summer day several members of a herd may be seen wallowing and kicking at the air with outstretched legs.

A shaman offers thanks to the Great Spirit after a successful buffalo hunt.

One might imagine a Vision Quest overlooking the foothills and Peigan teepees, crowned by the majestic Rocky Mountains.

Hunting methods are thought to have been handed down from ancient times and further perfected with each generation. Not much is known about the Paleo-Indians who inhabited the prairies some ten to twelve thousand years ago, but archaeological evidence suggests that they were superb hunters of, among other animals, prehistoric musk-ox and woolly mammoths. Bison seem to have been the only prehistoric North American mammal killed communally.

The Blackfoot Confederacy

The Blackfoot peoples, once referred to as "Lords of the Plains," have been traced back about a thousand years by archaeologists, but their early historical record is vague. By the 1700s, the Blackfoot realm extended from the foothills of the Rocky Mountains to the current Alberta-Saskatchewan border, and from the North Saskatchewan River to the Missouri River in present-day Montana. The Blackfoot were one of the most feared and respected warrior nations, and over the years fought many of their neighbors, including Cree, Assiniboine, Sioux, and Crow tribes.

The Blackfoot Confederacy consisted of three main tribes, all of Algonquian linguistic stock: the Blackfoot (Siksika), the Blood (Kainai), and the Peigan and North Peigan (Pekuni). Each tribe had its own chief.

In 1877, after the signing of Treaty Seven, the Blackfoot settled into reserves. The buffalo had all but disappeared.

The tribe most clearly associated with Head-Smashed-In Buffalo Jump is the Peigan (pronounced pay-gan), once known as the Apiku'ni, meaning "badly tanned hides." The Peigan are thought to have settled the area around Brocket, Alberta (the historical record is unclear), as it was known to be a choice wintering site for buffalo. The present Peigan reservation is situated directly across the road from Head-Smashed-In Buffalo Jump. Today, Alberta's Peigan tribe has approximately 2,800 members, but in 1898 the tribe's population numbered only 536, a result of epidemics in the mid-1800s.

The tribes of the Blackfoot Confederacy had a sociological hierarchy based on age and maturity. The youngest members of the Peigan tribe were known as Pigeons. Pigeons who successfully achieved a sense of strength through a vision quest would be upgraded to Mosquito status. The next three levels were Brave (or Brave-Dog), Crazy-Dog, and the prominent Kit-Fox. Chiefs came from the Kit-Fox class. Elderly tribesmen became Bulls. The buffalo bull was thought to have given these men strength, endurance, and the power to trample their enemies. Women belonged to a variety of societies, one of which was known as the Matoki class, or Buffalo Society.

Explorers such as Louis-Joseph Gaultier de La Vérendrye were astonished to discover that Blackfoot tribes moved across the prairie in perfectly regimented order. Three separate files—wives; men and young women; and children and old men—searched for the elusive buffalo in times of need. Advance scouts were sent out to look for either buffalo or the enemy, whichever came first. Warriors and medicine men brought up the rear of the advancing columns. Women and horse- or dog-drawn travois carried the tribe's belongings, including dismantled teepees and extra firewood. Utensils were stuffed in parfleches (bags made from buffalo rawhide).

Native boys learned to hunt buffalo by chasing buffalo calves. When the boys became braves, the hunt became more serious. A great amount of knowledge and skill was involved.

Buffalo bulls were in better condition than the females in the spring, so spring hunts could not be ruled out. But the cows were at their worst, as many were pregnant or lactating. Early Native hunters no doubt came to understand the varying nutritional conditions of their quarry. Explorers like David Thompson knew to seek out the fattest animals. Protein starvation was not uncommon at the time, and it was valuable to know that buffalo meat taken in the fall had almost five times the nutritional value as the same amount taken in the spring.

Communal hunts took place throughout the year, but the females and young were in prime physical condition in the autumn. The animals were fat from grazing all summer long, and their hides were thicker as well.

Between the autumn and spring hunting seasons, early communal hunters found it advantageous to kill members of the nursery herds, which consisted of adult cows, male and female yearlings, and young calves. The bulls were safely out of the way and the young buffalo, always together, were natural candidates for the buffalo jump.

Cows calve in spring, though some have been known to give birth as late as July. At birth the single calves (rarely twins) are a rough-looking reddish brown and weigh between 14–32 kilograms (30–70 pounds). Their horns protrude when they are only two months old.

The cows' behavior becomes erratic when they wander off to "drop" their young. The calves are understandably weak and wobbly at birth, but they learn to walk within a few hours. They are weaned at seven months and feed on prairie grasses for the rest of their lives. Buffalo parents care for their young, often huddling together to protect them from predators or bad weather.

Bulls tend to keep to themselves until mating season, and the older cows are generally the herd leaders. Bulls will herd in groups of five to ten, but some are loners. Young bulls reach maturity at about six years and cows at four years, both sexes living as long as thirty years. Some cows have been known to produce young even in the final years of their lives.

Bison mate in mid-summer. A harem of cows is

Competing male buffalo butt their heads together, often rolling and dusting between attacks.

The sprawling base of the main kill site ... could this be "where he got his head smashed in"?

When bulls were safely out of the way, mothers and calves were candidates for the buffalo jump.

8

gathered by each bull, and when a lone, unclaimed cow is discovered by more than one bull, a furious encounter takes place. Like male bighorn sheep, the competing male buffalo violently butt their heads together, often rolling and dusting between attacks. The combatants stare each other down and paw at the earth before lashing their tails, bucking, and savagely charging with low, guttural bellows. Some duels last more than half an hour, and bulls may become so agitated from the rut that they will not eat for days. The weaker bull may fall to his knees in submission or reel away in anger, but battles are rarely fatal. Cows do not always stick around to see the winner. In fact they may well leave with a third party.

The Fatal Precipice

A tribe's medicine man predicted the arrival of the buffalo by performing a mystical ritual with an *iniskin*, or buffalo stone. This *iniskin* was usually a crudely carved piece of ammonite (the fossil shell of an extinct mollusk from the Cretaceous period). Small lumps of flint or quartzite were also used. Some of these rocks were actually shaped like bison. Elders prayed over the *iniskin*, but the ochre-smeared stone was the property of the medicine man and was stored in his medicine bundle. At a crucial point in the ceremony, the medicine man would raise the stone and grip it tightly as he uttered a solemn prayer, then he would drop it quietly to the earth.

Legend has it that the first *iniskin* revealed itself

A dramatic replica of the fatal precipice looms above a mock archaeological dig site.

to a Blackfoot woman. The stone was wedged in the fork of a cottonwood tree. It issued forth a number of songs in the sound of a bird chirping, and these songs cast spells over the bison.

Following a successful *iniskin* ceremony, the best runners were chosen to chase the buffalo from the open prairie to the gathering area. The rolling Porcupine Hills provided natural confinement areas and a number of routes to the jumps.

According to Peigan legend, thousands of years ago the tribe's ancestors subsisted on berries, roots, birds, and small animals. Enormous buffalo herds roamed the plains, but they were not hunted, as these huge, horned mammals were known to brutally attack and devour tribesmen. Then one day while travelling across the prairies, Napi, the Blackfoot creator, saw several human bodies lying dead, dismembered and partly eaten by buffalo. The Natives were his children, his dearest creation, and the terrible sight saddened him. "This will not do," Napi declared. "I will change this. The people shall eat the buffalo."

As the Trickster, Napi led the herds to the Porcupine Hills of southern Alberta, and here he fashioned weapons for the people to use against the buffalo. But the tribesmen were puzzled by such innovative weapons and uncertain how to use them, so Napi gathered his children and revealed the *pis'kun* (buffalo jump) method of killing the previously invincible buffalo. He also showed the Natives how to use flakes of sharp-edged stone to remove the animals' hides.

The mythologies of various tribes explain the origins of the buffalo jump. Crow legends suggest that they were the first to use the buffalo jump method of slaughtering bison. According to Joseph Medicine Crow, a revered Montana Crow storyteller, there came a time when Old Man Coyote (the Crows' creator) and his people were hungry. The crafty Coyote chose a running site near a cliff wall, then challenged the buffalo to a race. The buffalo accepted the challenge. Old Man Coyote was ahead in the race and took advantage of the buffalo by hiding at the lower end of the jump, thus tricking the herd over the precipice and providing the tribe with meat for many days.

Whatever its origin, there is archaeological proof that the buffalo jump was part of the Native way of life for over ten thousand years, and that Head-Smashed-In Buffalo Jump was still in use as recently as 150 years ago.

There are more than one hundred prehistoric buffalo jumps found across North America, but Head-Smashed-In, located 4.8 kilometres (3 miles) north of the Oldman River on the southeastern edge of the Porcupine Hills, is the best preserved of these sites.

In 1998, 728 hectares (1800 acres) of grassland around Head-Smashed-In was designated as a Provincial Historical Resource. The actual UNESCO World Heritage Site encompasses some 162 hectares (400 acres). It is hoped the designation will protect Head-Smashed-In's fragile ecosystem from industrial development.

The gathering basin at Head-Smashed-In is surrounded by high ground. The entire valley is approximately 35 square kilometres (13.5 square miles) in size. In theory, several herds—possibly hundreds of animals—could have been gathered here to await slaughter. There is no way for archaeologists to tell just how many bison were killed in a single jump.

V-shaped drive lanes are visible all over the valley, each lane marked off with cairns positioned 5–6 metres (16–20 feet) apart. These cairns were known as "dead men" by early European explorers. A drive-lane cairn consisted of five to ten rocks clustered together and embedded in the ground. Braves wedged branches or brush from the coulee bottoms into some of the cairns in scarecrow-like form. The

constant wind at Head-Smashed-In kept the scarecrows moving and their dry-brush bodies rattling. Other cairns were occupied by people who waved buckskins or lit small buffalo-chip (dried dung) fires. These braves smeared a grease and sage concoction on their bodies to prevent the bison from detecting their human scent.

Tribesmen wrapped in buffalo or coyote robes would lure the herds forward in well-rehearsed decoy manoeuvres. These braves had to be highly fleet-footed.

Suddenly the hills would come alive with frightened, near-sighted buffalo stampeding down drive lanes lined with wild-brush scarecrows, fires, and yelling, hide-flapping tribesmen.

The drive lanes range in age from five hundred

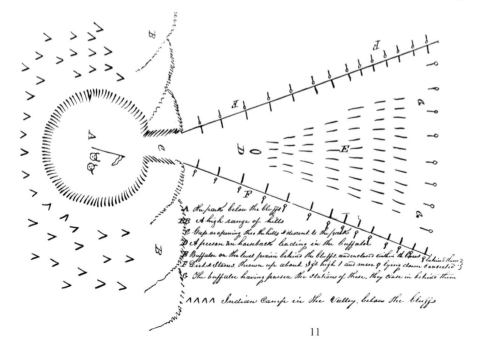

This drawing from 1854 shows how Natives used drive lanes to funnel the buffalo toward the cliff. Each of the crosses on the funnel edges represents a cairn of stones and sticks that tricked the near-sighted buffalo into thinking that they were people. Courtesy Glenbow Archives NA-3225-4.

to six thousand years old. Some of the rocks from the specific drive-lane cairns have been moved a kilometre or more from their original site, as the cairn stones from one drive lane were often taken to repair or build another. Additional lanes were sometimes added to handle the overflow of traffic.

Not all of the drive lanes in the Porcupine Hills led to the main jump site at Head-Smashed-In. Some lanes may have led to an old pound in the Olsen Creek valley. Many alternate lanes led buffalo to the Calderwood Jump, which was probably used as a kill site for smaller herds. Still other lanes led through the ravines of the Porcupine Hills to what may have been a network of lesser jumps.

One of the longest drive lanes behind Head-Smashed-In stretches 6.4 kilometres (4 miles) and contains over one thousand cairns. Rush or rawhide strips placed strategically in the stones would serve as "dead men" to stir up the herds.

The frenzied bison jammed together and thundered forward, funnelling down the lanes. Frantic herd leaders, grand matriarchs, may have sensed the danger of the trap, but it would have been too late to turn back. Adept Native warrior-hunters kept the animals in their lanes. Neighbouring tribes may have been called in to assist in the drive, as there would be plenty of meat for everyone. Buffalo who managed to escape one lane may have been rerouted down another.

It was imperative that none of the bison escaped alive, for the Native hunters strongly believed that the great animals could communicate their misadventures to other bison. If a few buffalo escaped, they might warn other herds of the Natives' trap.

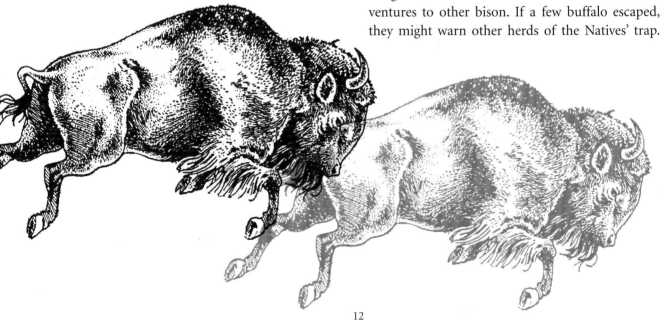

A mid-summer's view of the lower hiking trail leading up to the main jump at Head-Smashed-In.
Make sure you protect yourself from the sun when hiking these trails!

The Natives further believed that a bison herd should be slaughtered together so that they might be reincarnated as a complete herd—ready to be killed again.

Stampeding toward the cliff at speeds of up to 55 kilometres per hour (34 mph), the buffalo could not have known their fate. The prairie horizon was obscured by smoke from the hunters' fires and the dust churned up by the hundreds of hoofs violently striking the earth. One massive, powerful animal charged into the rear of another as the doomed legions pressed inescapably toward the fatal precipice.

One might assume that the name "Head-Smashed-In" refers to the unfortunate buffalo, but according to George Dawson, who worked for the Geological Survey of Canada in the 1880s, the name comes from an allegedly true story concerning a Peigan brave who wanted a closer look at the plummeting buffalo. The brave situated himself against the cliff wall, beneath the lip over which the bison charged. He watched from his privileged position as one after another the bison hurtled to their deaths. He was safe for a while, but the pile of bison carcasses grew much higher than he had anticipated, eventually pinning him against the cliff wall. When his fellow tribesmen came to butcher their kill, they were shocked to discover the young brave with his head crushed by the weight of dead and dying buffalo. In the Blackfoot language, this place is called *Estipah-Sikikini-Kots*, meaning "where he got his head smashed in."

A Successful Kill

Ghastly mounds of dead or stunned bison lay at the base of the buffalo jump following a kill. Many animals were simply wounded, with broken limbs or internal damage. Braves moved in to finish the job.

In the early years, lances or mauls (heavy hammers or clubs) were used on survivors' skulls. Slings also may have been used. In more recent centuries, arrows were fired at close range.

A successful hunt may have included two or three lesser drives, lasting several hours or perhaps even days. Anywhere from fifty to five hundred men, women, and children from the tribe participated.

The butchering and distribution of the buffalo carcasses was a communal operation. Autumn nights often brought early frost, and the Peigan

Teepees on the open Prairie near Head-Smashed-In herald mid-summer festivities at Pow Wow Days.

women had to work as quickly as possible to slit open the bellies of the dead bison, crack the ribs with mauls, remove the entrails, and drag the remains downwind from the awful stench of the kill. These gutted carcasses were hauled down the slopes, then raised on low platforms to keep the meat clean. The meat was butchered on the spot.

Preferred cuts of meat were awarded to the better hunters, and other choice cuts to their prominent relatives. Buffalo livers, brains, hearts, and kidneys were eaten raw at the kill site. Married women removed and ate the sacred buffalo tongues in thanksgiving. Hump fat was removed. Sweet-tasting marrow was carved out of the leg bones. (Marrow was considered a delicacy when preserved in a buffalo bladder.) The animals were cut into manageable pieces such as leg sections and racks of ribs. Smaller or broken ribs, vertebrae, pelvic bones, and most of the skulls were left behind. Cow-calf groups were the most desirable for butchering.

Of course the fresh meat would not keep for long, so pemmican was made by combining dried, lean meat with melted fat and pounding it into a paste. This ensured a nutritional food source through the winter. Pemmican could last up to two years if need be. If mold developed, the affected piece could be cut away like a piece of bad cheese. Pemmican was vital to the Natives' northern prairie existence, and the Hudson's Bay Company adopted pemmican as an essential survival food for its traders.

One explorer's favourite recipe called for 50 pounds of buffalo meat mixed with 20 pounds of hard fat and 20 pounds of soft fat. Meat strips were pounded out on a buffalo hide with rocks or sticks, then dried. Grease, tallow, marrow, saskatoon berries, chokecherries, and additional meat were crushed and mixed together. This buttery concoction was sewn up for storage in large sacks or buffalo bladders, with the air pockets pounded out to form a tighter seal.

One bison supplied enough meat to feed a tribe of approximately three hundred people for one day. Imagine how much food and leather a kill of two to three hundred buffalo would have supplied.

On hot, windless days the smell was terrible. Bodies had to cool before the hides could be stripped off and staked out on the ground or hung on drying racks. Select hides were scraped and prepared with a brain paste to make them pliable. They were then smoke cured. Scraped calf skins made good parfleches. These leather bags would be painted or decorated with beadwork. Bad skins were kept for rawhide. Bleached skulls were dotted with red ochre and kept for ceremonial purposes such as the Sun Dance, which was performed to ensure the return of the buffalo. Bison horns were used on a medicine man's headdress or carved into spoons and ladles. Children made toys from unused bones. Ribs were used as runners on children's sleds. Other bones were fashioned into fleshers, knives, awls, or gardening tools. Tails made excellent fly-swatters.

Water for boiling and rinsing was fetched from

nearby springs. Boiling stones were heated over buffalo-chip or wood fires while 0.5-metre-deep (1.5-foot) pits were dug in the ground and lined with buffalo hide, smooth side up. The pits were then filled with water and hot boiling stones were placed in the water to provide necessary heat for cooking. These boiling stones were cobblestones the size of small footballs and were probably carried up from the Oldman River bottom. Remnants of these stones now litter the base of Head-Smashed-In wherever you look.

Leg bones were smashed to bits and thrown into the cooking pot to draw out grease. It was a laborious task, producing only a cup of grease per cooking pot. For days fires and boiling pits were used throughout the processing area.

It was once estimated that the Indians had over three hundred separate uses for a buffalo. Hides were made into clothing or used to cover teepees and lodges. It took over thirty hides to cover

Saskatoon berries.

some council lodges and sixteen to twenty skins for a large teepee. Smaller sections of hide were fashioned into caps, moccasins, or leggings. Some hides were stitched together and stretched over bent willow branches to make "bull boats."

The list of items a buffalo carcass provided is long and varied, but included glue, whistles, shields, bowstrings, ropes, snowshoes, saddles, blankets, and robes. Buffalo robes protected the Natives from cold prairie winds while travelling. These robes were usually decorated with coloured lines or with pictographs denoting episodes of personal or tribal heroism. Buffalo robes and horses were the Natives' two most important bartering items.

The Blackfoot probably acquired their first horses through trades with southern tribes sometime around 1740. Previously unknown to the Blackfoot people, horses were called *po-no-kah-mita* by the Peigan, which means "elk dog" in their language. The horses were quickly incorporated into the hunting process and proved extremely useful.

Trained buffalo horses were among the fastest, most intelligent animals on the plains. They readily learned to charge the much-larger bison and to swerve as arrows flew from hunters' bowstrings.

Blackfoot braves rode bareback, controlling these "buffalo runners" by exerting pressure with their knees. Manoeuvring a buffalo horse required extraordinary skill, as wounded bulls were extremely dangerous to approach and gopher holes that randomly appeared in the prairie dirt threatened to throw both man and mount. Still, stories were told of daring braves who jumped on the backs of wild, running bison, speared select animals, and miraculously clambered back onto their horses.

Horses made it easier for hunters to control the buffalo herds. One resultant technique was known as the "surround." Native hunters on horseback would surround a herd and attack from all sides, yelling loudly as they tightened their circle around the bison. Mauls were used to finish off the wounded animals.

Another hunting technique used by the Natives was to herd the buffalo into "jumping pounds," corrals ranging in size from 55–114 metres (60–125 yards) across, with a drop of 1.8–2.4 metres (6–8 feet). The pounds were camouflaged with branches and twigs, and tribesmen herded the buffalo through the 9-metre-wide (10-yard) entrance. Once inside, the bison were promptly slaughtered. Hudson's Bay Company trader Peter Fidler witnessed a pound kill while visiting Peigan territory in 1797. He wrote, "The hatchet is frequently used and it is shocking to see the poor animals thus pent up

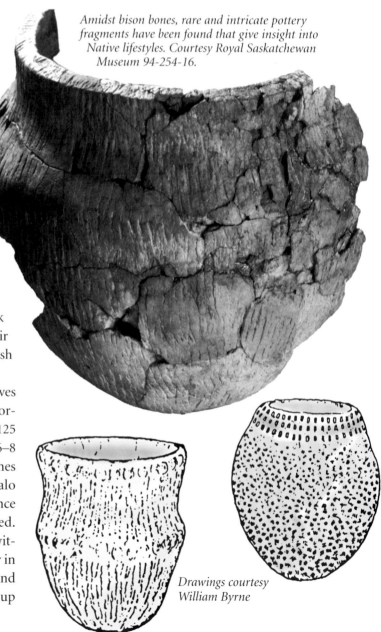

Amidst bison bones, rare and intricate pottery fragments have been found that give insight into Native lifestyles. Courtesy Royal Saskatchewan Museum 94-254-16.

Drawings courtesy William Byrne

without any way of escaping … Some with a stroke of an axe will open up nearly the whole side of a buffalo and the poor animal runs sometimes a considerable while all thro' the pound with its internals dragging on the ground and trod out by the others."

Whatever method was used, the buffalo hunt was serious business. Sport-hunting was taboo, and any brave caught straying for the glory of a solo kill would have his home burned or lose his favorite horse. Food and clothing were provided for every member of the tribe, including the aged and disadvantaged, and no one went without shelter.

The End of Plenty

At the beginning of the nineteenth century approximately 30 million buffalo dominated the plains, supporting an estimated 350,000 Indians. Seventy-five years later, carnal slaughter had reduced the bison population to near extinction. There is nothing in the annals of natural history to rival the massacre of these great animals.

In 1875 United States General Philip Sheridan supposedly told a Texas legislature worried about the bison's extinction: "The buffalo hunters have done in the last two years and will do more in the next year to settle the vexed Indian question than the entire regular army has done in the last thirty years. They are destroying the Indians' commissary, and it is a well-known fact that an army losing its base of supplies is placed at a great disadvantage.

Two and a half million bison were destroyed each year between 1870 and 1875. Homesteaders gathered the bones and hauled them to rail cars for much-needed extra income. Calcium from the bones was used for chalk and fertilizer. Courtesy Glenbow Archives NA-237-7.

Send them powder and lead, if you will; for the sake of lasting peace, let them kill, skin and sell until the buffaloes are exterminated."

The slaughter persisted unabated. Two and a half million bison were destroyed each year between 1870 and 1875. In one year the Santa Fe rail line shipped over 250,000 hides eastward. Homesteaders gathered the animals' bones and hauled them to the rail cars for much-needed extra income. Calcium from the bones was used for chalk and fertilizer.

Sport-hunting was in vogue, and one hunter of

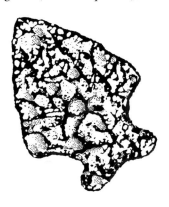

Buffalo peacefully grazing. The average buffalo weighs about 750 kilograms (over 1600 pounds).

the period reported, "I saw buffaloes lying dead on the prairie so thick that one could hardly see the ground. A man could have walked twenty miles upon those carcasses."

Popular hunting books of the 1870s and 1880s told sportsmen where to find the buffalo and how to shoot them. In his book *Prairie and Forest*, Parker Gillmore wrote, "The legitimate methods for their pursuit are by running them on horseback, when they are shot by a very large bored pistol as the sportsman ranges alongside, or to stalk them, a rifle of great power and caliber being then necessary. The shoulder-shot is the best, unless the animal happens to front you and expose his chest. Shooting at the head is a useless expenditure of ammunition, and, unless turned to charge, should never be attempted."

Smallpox and measles epidemics dramatically reduced the Indian population in the mid-1800s, and the diminishing plains bison herds wreaked further havoc, causing famine in many tribes. The Natives learned to hunt deer, elk, and antelope, and the Blackfoot made awkward attempts at vegetable cultivation, but by 1879 their situation was desperate. Tribes were at odds with each other over the lack of buffalo. Chiefs Sitting Bull, Poundmaker, and Crowfoot, of the Sioux, Cree, and Blackfoot, respectively, held two historic meetings to avert war. They finally agreed that the settlers were the problem.

Prairie fires raged in the late 1870s, sending the few remaining buffalo further south. Some of the Blackfoot blamed the spirit of the Sun. They believed that the Sun had opened up a hole in the Earth and driven the bison into the hole because the Sun was angry with the Natives for having traded with the white men.

Chief Crowfoot circa 1887.
Courtesy Glenbow Archives NA-29-1

By 1883, buffalo were virtually extinct in Montana, and those north of the forty-ninth parallel were not faring much better. The last recorded bison kill was in 1888. The North-West Mounted Police officially protected bison as of 1893, but the law was not well enforced until 1911. Only a few hundred plains bison existed in Canada at the turn of the century.

In 1907, seven hundred head of buffalo were sold to the Canadian government by a Montana rancher for $245 a head. These buffalo were the ancestors of the herd seen today at Elk Island National Park, in central Alberta. Since that time the buffalo have multiplied in captivity. Wood Buffalo National Park, Canada's largest national park, was established in 1922 to protect the wood bison subspecies (*bison athabascae*), but in 1925 some 6,673 plains bison (*bison bison*), some of them diseased, were brought in from the Wainwright compound. This resulted in a hybridization that almost destroyed the wood bison as a separate subspecies. Fortunately, pure wood bison specimens were discovered in 1957 and these were transported to the north shores of Great Slave Lake, where a healthy, expanding population now thrives.

THE ORIGIN OF THE BUFFALO

ONCE THE WORLD WAS ALMOST COMPLETE, CREATOR SUN AND MOTHER EARTH MADE TWO CHILDREN FOR THE LAND, MUDMAN AND RIBWOMAN. MUDMAN AND RIBWOMAN HAD MANY, MANY CHILDREN OF THEIR OWN, UNTIL THEY HAD TO START SPREADING OUT ACROSS THE LAND TO LOOK FOR FOOD AND FIND PLACES TO LIVE. BACK THEN, THERE WAS ONLY THE FOOD OF THE LAND TO EAT, LIKE BERRIES AND ROOTS. BUT IT DIDN'T TAKE LONG UNTIL THERE WERE TOO MANY PEOPLE TO LIVE OFF THE ROOTS AND BERRIES THAT THE LAND PROVIDED.

WHENEVER HE CAME DOWN FOR A VISIT, CREATOR SUN NOTICED THAT HIS CHILDREN AND THEIR CHILDREN KEPT GETTING THINNER. NOW THERE WAS NO DANGER OF THEM DYING, BECAUSE THE TIME HAD NOT YET COME FOR PEOPLE TO START GROWING OLD, BUT THEY WERE GOING HUNGRY, AND THAT BOTHERED CREATOR SUN.

ONE DAY, WHEN HE CAME DOWN TO VISIT HIS SON, MUDMAN, CREATOR SUN SAID TO MUDMAN, "LET'S GO FOR A WALK, YOU AND ME." SO THEY LEFT THE VILLAGE, AND WALKED INTO THE TALL GRASS THAT GREW ON THE PLAIN, UNTIL THEY CAME TO A CREEK. CREATOR SUN AND MUDMAN SAT DOWN

AT THE EDGE OF THE CREEK, AND CREATOR SUN BEGAN TO FORM THE MUD INTO A SHAPE HE'D BEEN THINKING ABOUT.

CREATOR SUN GAVE THE NEW CREATURE FOUR LEGS, WITH A THICK BODY AND A BIG HEAD. THEN HE BLEW HIS BREATH INTO THE ANIMAL'S NOSTRILS, AND TOLD HIM TO INHALE THE AIR OF THIS WORLD FROM THE FOUR DIRECTIONS OF THE WIND. THE ANIMAL CAME TO LIFE, AND BREATHED THE AIR. HE TRIED TO STAND, BUT WAS VERY WEAK AND HIS EFFORTS TO STAND TIRED HIM OUT, SO THAT HE HAD TO SLEEP.

WHILE HE WAS SLEEPING, CREATOR SUN TOOK ONE OF HIS RIBS OUT TO MAKE THE ANIMAL A MATE, SO THAT THEY COULD REPRODUCE AND PROVIDE FOOD FOR ALL MUDMAN'S CHILDREN AND GRANDCHILDREN. WHEN HE WAS FINISHED ALL HIS CREATING, CREATOR SUN TOLD MUDMAN THAT THEY WOULD CALL THE CREATURE "EYE-I-IN-NAWHW", WHICH MEANS "THE THING THAT CAN BE PEELED." THAT IS, THE SKIN OF THE BUFFALO HAD TO BE PEELED OFF SO THAT THE PEOPLE COULD GET AT THE MEAT UNDERNEATH. ONCE THEY HAD BEEN NAMED, THE FIRST TWO BUFFALOES WALKED OFF TO EAT THE TALL, LUSH GRASS. CREATOR SUN TOLD MUDMAN THAT NOBODY WAS ALLOWED TO EAT ANY OF THE "EYE-I-IN-NAWHW" UNTIL THERE WERE ENOUGH OF THEM TO FEED ALL THE PEOPLE.

WITH ALL THE PRAIRIE GRASS, IT DIDN'T TAKE LONG FOR THE BUFFALO TO MULTIPLY THEMSELVES EVEN FASTER THAN MUDMAN AND RIBWOMAN'S CHILDREN. WHEN THERE WERE ENOUGH BUFFALO, CREATOR SUN TOLD MUDMAN THAT THE PEOPLE WERE ALLOWED TO EAT THE "EYE-I-IN-NAWHW", AND TO GROW STRONG AND PROSPER.

BUT THE PEOPLE NEEDED NAPI TO SHOW THEM HOW TO HUNT AND KILL THE BUFFALO, WHICH IS A STORY FOR ANOTHER PLACE ...

Story based on "Creator Sun's Gift of Food to His Children", taken from *The Sun Came Down: The History of the World as My Blackfeet Elders Told It* by Percy Bullchild.

PART TWO

UNEARTHING THE PAST

Early Digs and the Reeves' Phases

Junius B. Bird became the first archaeologist to dig at the Head-Smashed-In site when he was commissioned by the American Museum of Natural History in 1938. Bird's findings spurred further interest, and by 1949, Boyd Wettlaufer of the University of New Mexico had excavated a series of 3.7-metre-deep (12-foot) trenches at the Head-Smashed-In kill site, which had once been a prime butchering spot. Wettlaufer's notation "N.M.U.–1949," painted on the cliff wall near the main kill area, can still be seen.

Boyd Wettlaufer was a dedicated archaeologist who worked on an extremely limited budget. Area ranch-owner Rose Dersch recalls Wettlaufer eating pigeons for weeks after his supplies were depleted.

The Province of Alberta erected a cairn to commemorate Wettlaufer's work, but was forced to remove the stone marker because it attracted pothunters (illegal artifact collectors).

Theft and vandalism are always a problem on archaeological sites. Work by the Glenbow Foundation's Dr. Richard G. Forbis was thwarted by vandalism and random amateur digging. Forbis attempted to keep his site a secret, but by 1964 an area 1–1.5 metres (3–5 feet) deep, covering 465 square metres (5,000 square feet), had been stripped of priceless artifacts. In an attempt to prevent further loss, the Province of Alberta made Head-Smashed-In a Provincial Historical Site in 1979.

Dr. Brian (Barney) Reeves joined Dr. Forbis in

The Calderwood excavation site in the 1980s.

the 1960s, and they received valuable assistance and land donations from two local ranchers, Dr. Alex Calderwood and Walter Dersch (both now deceased). Dersch pointed out drive lanes to Forbis and Reeves, and donated 0.4 hectares (1 acre) of land for their use. The Calderwoods donated 4.9 hectares (12 acres) in 1968, including the land on which the museum now stands.

Dr. Reeves' digs varied in depth from 0.6–10.7 metres (2–35 feet). These excavations were generally done by horizontal shovel work and screening. These digs focused on three areas located to the north, south, and east of the main jump site. The more plentiful material from the 8-metre (26-foot) level dated back to about 1000 B.C., and Reeves and crew were confident that the bottom strata would prove to be considerably older.

Data collected from stratigraphic layers of earth and rock in the northern and southern parts of Head-Smashed-In, including the Calderwood Jump, offered proof of major differences in Native cultural levels over a period of about 5,500 years. Radiocarbon techniques were used to date charred bone, whole bone, charcoal, and collagen (proteins found in connective tissues such as skin, ligaments, tendons, bone, and cartilage).

Results turned up eighteen different radiocarbon dates, which were divided into five cultural periods named by Dr. Reeves:

The *Mummy Cave Complex* (3600 B.C. to 3100 B.C.) yields side-notched projectile points, bone tools, and microcrystalline flakes. (The discovery of this oldest phase proved that Head-

a.) The trail from Head-Smashed-In leads to a "sampling site" circa 1986. b.) All digs are carefully measured and documented for archaeological records. c.) Archaeologists spend hours bagging samples for closer scrutiny later.

Smashed-In is not as ancient as the Bonfire Shelter Jump in Texas, which is over ten thousand years old. The largest known jump is the Highwood Buffalo Jump in Montana.)

The *Pelican Lake Phase* (900 B.C. to A.D. 100–300) reveals a series of superimposed kills with bones badly scattered. Tools found at this level included many styles of points used on long darts, bifaces (drills or knives), scrapers, retouched flakes, choppers, bone-mashers, anvils, and hammers. Paleozoic cherts (flintlike rock used to make tools) from southwestern British Columbia and Montana suggest the early Natives travelled and traded extensively.

The *Besant Phase* (approximately A.D. 200) was a brief one. Findings consisted primarily of Knife River flint, which originated in the North Dakota area and was brought here through trade with other tribes.

The *Avonlea Phase* (A.D. 100–300 to A.D. 850) contains the first evidence of massive bison drives. Charred bones and fire-broken boiling stones were found, and Avonlea points, atlatl dart points, stemmed arrow points, and the usual lithics (stone tools and weapons) were unearthed in great abundance.

The *Old Women's Phase* (A.D. 850 to A.D. 1850) provides additional proof of successive bison slaughters. Charred and heated bone (including human bone), hair, horn, sheaths, and manure were discovered. Bifaces became smaller. Trade artifacts and steel arrowheads were also exhumed.

a.) Close-up of various types of buffalo bones unearthed. b.) A view of the main kill precipice from the top of the Interpretive Centre. c.) Archaeologists sift through smaller artifacts, searching for clues about early hunters.

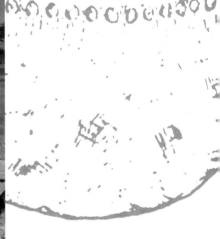

The main sampling site (circa 1987). Jack Brink and his crew work as tourists stroll down from Head-Smashed-In to have a look.

For reasons as yet unknown, the Natives did not use the jump from about 3100 B.C. to 900 B.C. By 100 A.D. large blocks of bedrock had collapsed from the cliff wall sending sandstone debris across the killing area.

According to Dr. Reeves' findings, the complex, mysterious operations of early Natives at Head-Smashed-In indicate that the buffalo drives began in the middle centuries of the third millennium B.C., nearly one thousand years before the pyramids were erected in ancient Egypt.

In addition to the plethora of bones, tools and potsherds, prehistoric sites at Head-Smashed-In include burial camps, eagle-trapping pits, over one thousand drive-lane cairns, a vision-quest site, pictographs, teepee rings, and burial rocks. Archaeologists must decipher the jumbled puzzle to understand how the early Natives lived and precisely how they used the buffalo jump. Some of the unearthed material has been buried for thousands of years, and before it was buried it lay exposed to the elements for perhaps hundreds of years more.

The exact section of the kill site that was used by Natives is a relatively narrow deposit that could be depleted by extensive digging. Archaeologists are saving parts of the site for future scientific work with improved technologies.

At the Butchering Site

The main processing or butchering site was the focus of work by senior archaeologist Jack Brink of the Archaeological Survey of Alberta. Brink and associates spent nine years (1983–91) examining the approximately 1-square-kilometre (245-acre) site. Brink's results suggest that the Natives may have found working directly below the cliff too cramped and putrid, and they may have dragged the meat down the slopes to flat areas, where they could butcher more easily and avoid the stench of the main kill site. The smell of rotting flesh quickly became a factor in the summer, with daytime temperatures reaching 31 degrees Celsius (88 F).

It is a common misconception that the deeper an article is buried, the older it is. Crews digging on the processing flats discovered five to six thousand-year-old material at a depth of only 10–20 centimetres (4–8 inches). The closer one gets to the cliff, the greater the deposition of cultural material and the deeper it is buried. In the 1960s, Reeves and crew dug to depths of 9–12 metres (30–40 feet) to reveal bones, tools, and weapons approximately five thousand years old.

In the processing area, boiling stones, whole or fragmented, combine with smashed buffalo bones to form an unearthly pavement, testimony to the thousands of long-boiling pit fires that burned here.

Boiling stones have characteristic fractures not unlike arrowheads or stones used for tools. The intense heat and repeated use of these rocks caused predictable cracks and fissures.

Metallic points, knives, bucket fragments, and glass beads discovered in the processing area indicate that the jump was still in use at a time when Europeans were trading with the Indians. Other tools and materials suggest Native processes for grease and marrow extraction, meat stripping and drying, pemmican-making, hide treatment, and so on.

The long humerus bone was a favourite of the early plains people. The proximal end (nearest the body) is soft, spongy, and rich in grease, whereas the distal end (furthest from the body) is extremely hard and undesirable to eat. Archaeologists found

Interpretive Centre close-up of simulated dig pit complete with note pad and archaeologists' "tools of the trade".

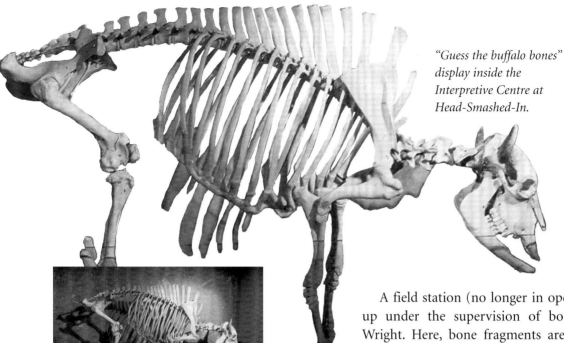

"Guess the buffalo bones" display inside the Interpretive Centre at Head-Smashed-In.

forty-one humerus distal ends without their opposing proximal ends. (But scientists are aware that nature may play tricks on them. For example, the Natives may not have preferred specific types and parts of bones. Perhaps the softer sections simply decayed more rapidly. Perhaps insects or other animals consumed these missing sections. All possible explanations must be carefully examined.)

Sites are not rated as better or worse than other sites. All finds are important. Likewise, a small site may reveal more significant material than a larger site.

A field station (no longer in operation) was set up under the supervision of bone expert Milt Wright. Here, bone fragments are identified and compared to bones from a complete bison skeleton. Wright determines which parts of the bone are missing or damaged and how this may relate to Paleo-Indian butchering patterns. Specimens are then catalogued.

Each piece of bone is assigned a catalogue number, then individually wrapped in tinfoil (later transferred to a plastic bag). The recorded information includes the location, the excavation unit, and the depth at which the bone was found. Between two and three thousand sets of new information were recorded in this manner each summer at Head-Smashed-In, up until the mid-1990s, when active excavations stopped. All data was filed on computer at the museum laboratory and was ultimately transferred via computer to the

Alberta Department of Community Development in Edmonton.

The type of excavation work done at Head-Smashed-In was known as "sampling." By testing various sectors of a site, archaeologists arrive at essential bison demographics: how many animals were killed over a given period of time, sex and age ratios, etc. It is difficult to determine how many bison died during a single drive, as many drives may have taken place at one jump over a relatively short span of time.

There is no evidence of other animals, such as elk or deer, being run off the cliffs at either the Head-Smashed-In or Calderwood Jumps.

Head-Smashed-In offers an unparalleled record of the early people of the plains. The detailed records provided through excavation of bone beds

Milt Wright hard at work cataloguing bison bones (circa 1986).

and analysis of stone weapons and tools led to Head-Smashed-In Buffalo Jump's designation as a UNESCO World Heritage Site in 1981.

The Calderwood Jump

Located at the northeastern tip of the Porcupine Hills, the Calderwood jump site boasts a largely undisturbed campsite and butchering area. There is more toppled bedrock here than at Head-Smashed-In, and this slump material may have helped trap wounded bison.

The jump is named for the Calderwood family of Granum, Alberta, who donated the land in 1968. The surrounding area provides ample evidence of an intricate system of drive lanes.

Sue Marshall and crew, under the direction of Jack Brink, dug various test sites at Calderwood. In the initial pits, bone appeared at the 10–15 centimetre (4–6 inch) level. This bone was radiocarbon dated at about two hundred years old. Three separate bone layers have now been tested, with the oldest samples dating back twenty-eight hundred to three thousand years.

A limited number of lithics were also found, including chert, quartzite and obsidian flakes, a quartzite side-scraper, and a few points. Buffalo skulls, teeth, vertebrae, and pelvic bones appear in abundance.

The dead-end valleys, slopes, and channelling points only a kilometre away at Head-Smashed-In could have easily provided a "commuter" access route to the Calderwood Jump.

The entrance to Head-Smashed-In Interpretive Centre.

PART THREE

HEAD-SMASHED-IN TODAY

In 1984, a special sod-turning ceremony launched Head-Smashed-In's multi-million-dollar interpretive centre project. A team of ten archaeologists then set to work exhuming any valuable archaeological material located on the site designated for the museum and parking lot. This work was completed in time for the centre's opening on July 23, 1987.

During the opening ceremony a Peigan chief blessed the site in his native tongue. Andrew and Sarah, the Duke and Duchess of York, attended and were presented with a buffalo head and a Native painting depicting the jump in use. Various government officials welcomed thousands of visitors from around the world.

The museum and parking lot are removed from view to allow the seven-tiered interpretive centre to blend naturally with the surrounding Porcupine Hills. Much of the centre is below ground level.

Each level of the interpretive centre offers a trip through time. Fascinating murals depict the lives of the buffalo and the Plains Indians who hunted them. A ten-minute documentary film *In Search of the Buffalo* is screened in the eighty-seat theatre. There are dramatic audio-visual displays, realistic dioramas of how the jump site works, full-scale archaeological pits, and three mighty bison about to take a 10-metre (33-foot) plunge. The cliff these bison stand upon is actually a fibreglass mould taken from the Calderwood Jump.

LEVEL ONE, "Uncovering the Past," explains the delicate ecological balance of the prehistoric plains and the Porcupine Hills. The geography, flora and fauna, climatic conditions, and the anthropology of the early Native people are examined.

LEVEL TWO, "Napi's People," looks at the Plains Indians' lifestyle. Numerous period artifacts are on display, along with a full-size travois and teepee. (Watch out for the lone bison lurking by the staircase!) Parts of this display are hands-on: a buffalo robe can be touched, and the teepee and its Native contents can be closely examined.

LEVEL THREE is "The Buffalo Hunt." Buffalo characteristics and behaviour are discussed and models of a gathering basin, its drive lanes and jump are presented. In addition, the visitor can become acquainted with the early Natives' spiritual beliefs and traditions.

Prince Andrew and Sarah Ferguson, the Duke and Duchess of York, are escorted by a Peigan Chief at the opening ceremonies of Head-Smashed-In on 23 July 1987.

LEVEL FOUR, "Cultures in Contact," covers the arrival of the European settlers, fur traders, and trappers, with emphasis on their effect upon Native culture. A startling pile of buffalo skulls provides a grim reminder of the great bisons' slaughter to near extinction in the late nineteenth century.

LEVEL FIVE has a display that deals with the exacting science of archaeology. A slide show covering archaeology and Head-Smashed-In Buffalo Jump can be viewed in the special screening theatre. Visitors used to be able to peer through a large laboratory window and witness professionals processing ancient artifacts, but this area is no longer in use.

The centre has a well-stocked bookstore and a shop that sells souvenirs and Peigan crafts. A sixty-seat cafeteria is located off the second-floor gallery. Washrooms are available and wheelchairs are provided for people with reduced mobility.

Trails lead from the interpretive centre to a panoramic vista overlooking the actual cliffs of Head-Smashed-In Buffalo Jump. Bluebunch fescue covers the gathering basin and, depending on the season and the amount of moisture, wheatgrass-bromeweed and wheatgrass-needlegrass may be seen among indigenous shrubs and grasses blanketing the slopes and coulees.

Most of the area below the cliffs is covered with mixed prairie grasses. Valleys contain pockets of wild rye, vetch, marsh reed grass, and cow parsnip. Wildflowers may include early yellow locoweed,

Imagine thundering herds of bison stampeding toward the main "kill cliffs." Take the trail and explore the fascinating legacy of Head-Smashed-In Buffalo Jump.

A real-life sampling of buffalo skulls that are on display at the Interpretive Centre.

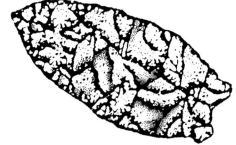

white camas, shooting star, and prickly wild roses. A springhead below the main kill area feeds shrubs such as the saskatoon berry, gooseberry, choke-cherry, bunchberry, and western snowberry.

Wildlife is rarely spotted at Head-Smashed-In, except by visitors who arrive at dawn or leave at dusk. (Rocky Mountain sunsets are worth the wait.) Mule deer, pronghorn antelope, elk, coyotes, marmots, and ground squirrels are all indigenous to the area. Wapiti, bighorn sheep, red squirrels, lynx, and the occasional cougar have been sighted in the far reaches of the Porcupine Hills. Garter snakes are the only snake species represented at Head-Smashed-In, but over thirty bird species have been sighted here, including redtailed hawks, cliff swallows, ruffed grouse, saw-whet owls, and mourning doves.

Guided tours begin May 1 and run until the end of the summer season. Tour hours are from 9 A.M. to 6 P.M. Winter hours are from 10 A.M. to 5 P.M. The museum is open all year.

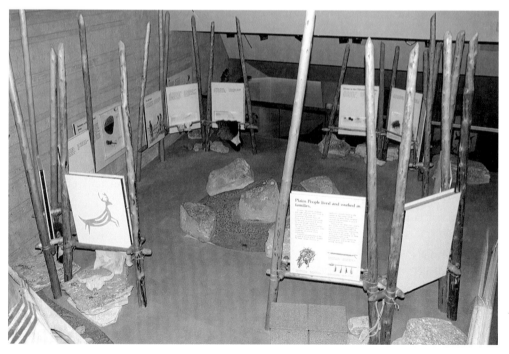

There are many fascinating displays to explore at Head-Smashed-In.

Lower trails lead to the camp and processing park of the site, where significant archaeological excavation has been done. These dig sites are no longer active, and lie waiting for better exploration techniques than currently exist.

Atop the highest point of the surrounding Porcupine Hills stands a pair of vision-quest structures. These prehistoric sites consist of ovals measuring 2 by 1.5 metres (7 by 5 feet). The sandstone blocks are piled about 40 centimetres (16 inches) high. These sites were once used for religious and ceremonial activities.

The Porcupine Hills are underlain by sandstone, shale, and siltstone beds. The broad, sloping hills end abruptly at Cretaceous bedrock, exposing stratified layers in the southwest and southeast. The coulees were scooped out by the Laurentide glacier over fourteen thousand years ago. Trout and Willow Creeks were formed, emptying into the Oldman River. Deep bedrock channels are now exposed on the eastern side at the Calderwood Jump site.

A Table Rock "burial ground" is situated on sacred Peigan land southwest of Head-Smashed-In and is not open to the public. Old tribal customs called for platform burials in trees, but this ancient block of bedrock offered a natural solution to the lack of trees. Offerings were left there to appease the spirits. Archaeologists are not sure if Table Rock is connected with the operation of the buffalo jump, but copper bracelets, turquoise-coloured glass beads, and skeletal remains have been found by archaeolo-

gists at the base of the rock, and it is thought to have been used as a burial site by the Natives for thousands of years.

Every grain of soil and pollen, every broken arrowhead, every small scrap of bone at Head-Smashed-In has a story to tell and may provide an answer to the many mysteries still puzzling archaeologists.

Site administrators and the Peigan people hope that the future generations of people who travel many miles to visit the interpretive centre will be moved by the dramatic history of Head-Smashed-In and will become involved in its promotion and preservation.

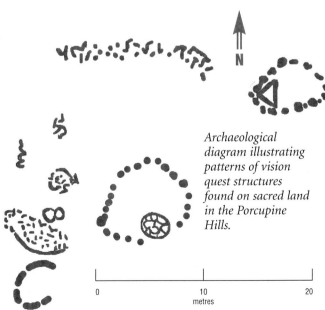

Archaeological diagram illustrating patterns of vision quest structures found on sacred land in the Porcupine Hills.

Atop the highest point of the surrounding Porcupine Hills stands a pair of vision-quest structures. These prehistoric sites consist of ovals measuring 2 by 1.5 metres (7 by 5 feet). The sandstone blocks are piled about 40 centimetres (16 inches) high. These sites are sacred and were once used for religious and ceremonial activities.

BIBLIOGRAPHY

Andkrist, Ralph K. *The Last Days of the Plains Indian*. Collier Books, 1963.

Barnett, Donald C. *Poundmaker (The Canadians)*. Fitzhenry & Whiteside Ltd., 1976.

Beaty, Chester B. *The Landscapes of Southern Alberta*. University of Lethbridge, 1975.

Bell, Dr. Charles N. *The Journal of Henry Kelsey 1691–1692*. Historical & Scientific Society of Manitoba, 1928.

Billard, Jules B. (editor). *The World of the American Indian*. National Geographic Society, 1974.

Brink, Jack, et al. Various preliminary reports, handbooks & journals on Head-Smashed-In & Calderwood Buffalo Jumps. Archaeological Survey of Alberta, 1979–1986.

Burland, Cottie. *North American Indian Mythology*. Paul Hamlyn Ltd., 1965.

Burpee, Lawrence J. *Pathfinders of the Great Plains*. Glasgow, Brook & Co., 1915.

Burpee, Lawrence J. & Arthur G. Doughty (editors). *The Makers of Canada*, Parkman Edition, Volume 21, 1911.

Cook, John R. *The Border and the Buffalo*. Topeka Books, 1907.

Cowie, Issac. *The Company of Adventurers: Hudson's Bay Reminiscence, 1867–74*. Toronto, 1913.

Crow, Joseph Medicine. "The Crow Indian Buffalo Jump Legends" (Symposium on Buffalo Jumps). Montana Archaeological Society Memoir, No. 1, May 1962.

Dewdney, Selwyn. *They Shared To Survive*. Macmillan of Canada Ltd., 1975.

Dorsey, George A. *The Pawnee: Mythology* (Part One). Carnegie Institution of Washington, 1906.

Doughty, A. G. & Chester Martin (editors). "The Kelsey Papers." Ottawa, 1929.

Erdoes, Richard. *The Sun Dance People: The Plains Indians, Their Past and Present*. Alfred A. Knopf, Inc., 1972.

Fisher, Olive M. & Clara L. Tyner. *Totem, Tipi, and Tumpline: Stories of Canadian Indians*. J. M. Dent & Sons, 1955.

Forbis, Richard G. "A Stratified Buffalo Kill in Alberta" & "Early Man and Fossil Bison," *Science* CXXIII, February, 1956.

Frison, George C. *Prehistoric Hunters of the High Plains*. Academic Press, 1978.

Gillmore, Parker. *Prairie and Forest*. Harper & Bros., 1874.

Grinnell, George Bird. *Blackfoot Lodge Tales: The Story of a Prairie People*. Great Britain, 1892.

Haines, Francis. *The Plains Indians: Their Origins, Migrations and Cultural Development*. Thomas Y. Crowell Co., 1976.

Hamilton, Charles (editor). *The American Indians' Own Story*. The Macmillan Co., 1957.

Helgason, Gail. *The First Albertans*. Lone Pine Publishing, 1987.

Hunt, Norman Bancroft & Werner Forman. *The Indians of the Great Plains*. Orbis Publishing Ltd., 1981.

Hungry Wolf, Adolf. *The Good Medicine Book*. Warner Paperback Library, 1973.

Jenness, Diamond. "Indians of Canada," National Museum of Canada Bulletin 15. Ottawa, 1932.

Jenness, Eileen. *The Indian Tribes of Canada*. Ryerson Press, 1933.

Letters & Notes on the North American Indians (8th ed., 2 vols.). London, 1851.

Long Lance, Buffalo Child. *Chief Buffalo Child Long Lance*. New York, 1928.

Miers, Earl S. (editor). *Indians of the Northern Plains*. G.P. Putnam's Sons, 1969.

Miller, Alfred J. *Braves and Buffalo: Plains Indian Life in 1837*. University of Toronto Press, 1973.

Moore, T. A. (editor). *Alberta Archaeology: Prospect and Retrospect*. Archaeological Society of Alberta, 1981.

Park, Ed. *The World of the Bison*. J. B. Lippincott Co., 1969.

Reeves, B. O. K. "Six Millenniums of Buffalo Kills," *Scientific American*, October 1983.

Roe, F. G. *The North American Buffalo*. Toronto, 1951.

Spalding, David A. E. *A Nature Guide to Alberta*. Hurtig Publishers, 1980.

Spence, Lewis. *North American Indians*. George G. Harrap & Co., 1914.

Symington, Fraser. *The Canadian Indian*. McClelland & Stewart, 1969.

Updike, Lee R. *Our People: Indians of the Plains*. Western Producer Prairie Books, 1972.

Newspapers: *Calgary Herald, Lethbridge Herald, Fort Macleod Gazette, The Albertan, Calgary Sun*.

Magazines: *Western Report, Canadian Geographic, National Geographic, Equinox*.

GLOSSARY

Albino Buffalo: a sacred white buffalo considered to be a sign of great changes signifying the viewer's metaphorical "crossroad" of life or the fufillment of an ancient prophecy.

Archaeology: scientific study of people from the past by careful examination of their artifacts and personal features.

Atlatl: prehistoric weapon used to bring down bison or other large animals for a kill.

Blackfoot: a Native tribe in the Blackfoot Confederacy.

Blackfoot Confederacy: a collection of Native tribes within the same language group who co-operated for mutual benefit and defense. They lived in the plains and foothills of what is now southwest Alberta and northwest Montana.

Blood: a Native tribe of the Blackfoot Confederacy.

Buffalo Runner: skilled Natives on horseback who guided wounded buffalo bulls, when herding bison for an eventual kill.

Dead Men: name given by early European explorers for cairns used in most drive lanes at Head-Smashed-In.

Drive Lanes: routes specially marked by cairns (piles of rock) enabling Natives to direct bison over a designated cliff wall for eventual slaughter.

Iniskin: small rocks or bits of fossils that are shaped like animals and used by medicine men for sacred ceremonies or in medicine bundles.

Jumping Pounds: corrals used to herd and butcher the impounded bison.

Napi (the Trickster): the Great Spirit, a mythological creator of all the universe.

Old Man Coyote (and Old Woman Coyote): early Crow and Siksika legend about the creators of Native people, how they came to see visions and ultimately how they learned to die.

Peigan: a Native tribe of the Blackfoot Confederacy. This group is most closely associated with the buffalo jumping activities at Head-Smashed-In. (Also sometimes spelled Piegan.)

Pemmican: dried strips of buffalo meat (preserved or "cured") that could be stored and eaten later.

Piskun: Blackfoot word for a buffalo jump.

Radiocarbon Dating: a method used to date (approximately) bones and artifacts via the amount of atomic carbon degradation found and measured by scientific instruments.

Stratigraphic Layers: a term used for geological layers of rock, excavated in dig sites and studied by archaeologists.

Sun Dance Lodge: a ceremonial building reflecting the twenty-eight articulated parts of a buffalo; situated next to the forty to fifty foot tree (stripped of its branches) used in a Sun Dance ceremony.

Surround: hunting technique in which hunters on horseback surrounded bison and attacked them from all sides.

UNESCO World Heritage Site: Head-Smashed-In Buffalo Jump is one of over 300 fragile environments specially protected by the United Nations and preserved for all times.

Vision Quest: a rite in which a young Blackfoot would go alone and spend four days and nights without food or drink, stationed on the highest point of the vicinity; and generally seated inside a circular rock formation. They hoped to receive a sign or dream from the spirit world. A vision was thought to be a form of coming of age.

INDEX

ABOUT THE AUTHOR

This is Gordon Reid's second book about World Heritage sites. The first, *Dinosaur Provincial Park*, tells the fascinating story of a time when Alberta was ruled by dinosaurs. Both projects were supported with the generous assistance of the Royal Canadian Geographical Society.

ABOUT THE PARK

Hours of Operation:
Summer: 9 A.M. – 6 P.M.
Winter: 10 A.M. – 5 P.M.

Inquiries & tour reservations:
Head-Smashed-In Buffalo Jump
PO Box 1977
Fort Macleod, Alberta
T0L 0Z0

Web: http://www.head-smashed-in.com

Phone: 403-533-2731
Fax: 403-553-3141

Toll Free (Alberta only): 310-0000

E-mail: info@head-smashed-in.com

More information on World Heritage
   Sites: www.unesco.org

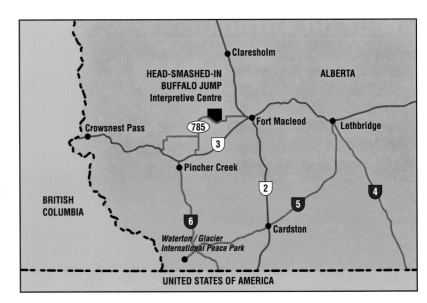